THE ART OF SUPPORTIVE LEADERSHIP

The *Art* of SUPPORTIVE LEADERSHIP

A Practical Handbook for People in Positions of Responsibility

J. Donald Walters

Crystal Clarity, Publishers
14618 Tyler Foote Road
Nevada City, California 95959

Cover design by Helen Strang

Fourth Printing, 1993

International Book Number 0-916124-20-7
Printed in the United States of America

"Where there is right action,
there is victory."

—Sanskrit proverb

CONTENTS

THE ART OF SUPPORTIVE LEADERSHIP

Chapter One

The Art of Leadership

Genuine leadership is of only one type: supportive. It leads people: It doesn't drive them. It involves them: It doesn't coerce them. It never loses sight of the most important principle governing any project involving human beings: namely, that *people are more important than things.*

Consider a situation in which none of the above statements might seem valid:

the battlefield. To a general, the most important thing, obviously, is victory. In the cause of victory he must commit men to possible, and sometimes even to certain, death. Is not victory, then — an abstraction, a thing — more important to him than the people he leads?

Yet the difference between great generals and mediocre ones may be attributed to the zeal great generals have been able to inspire in their men. Some excellent generals have been master strategists, and have won wars on this strength alone. Greatness, however, by very definition implies a great, an expanded view. It transcends intelligence and merely technical competence. It implies an ability to see the lesser in relation to the greater; the immediate in relation to the long term; the need for victory in relation to needs that will arise once victory has been achieved.

Leadership implies running at the head of the pack, and not driving it from behind. This is true also in military matters. Those who serve under a great general know well that he asks nothing of them that he would not first do himself. Such a general feels himself at one with his men, not superior to them. He knows that he and they are simply doing a job together.

A great general is a man of vision: necessarily so, for only with vision can he inspire his men to heroic action; only with vision can he make them desire victory as ardently as he does. He persuades them not by angry commands, but by the power of his own conviction. He involves others in his vision, and inspires them also to be visionaries.

People, even in warfare, are more important than things. Yet there are circumstances in which people can fulfill themselves perfectly only by total self-offering to whatever it is they believe in: times when great truths may be at stake, or when the safety of family or countrymen is threatened. There are times when, for the welfare of the greater number, individual lives must be sacrificed. The great general inspires in his soldiers, because he believes it also for himself, the realization that whatever may be demanded by the exigencies of war, death in a great cause is a life lived victoriously.

A great general is also loyal to his soldiers. Only in that spirit of loyalty does he demand loyalty of them in return.

Thus we see that even in critical times when stern command is necessary for proper leadership, the essence of genius in leadership is supportive, not dictatorial.

An example of a great general, though not always a great tactician, was George Washington. Rather than billet his tired and hungry soldiers on civilian homes, and rather than feed them by foraging, he chose — for himself as much as for his army — discomfort, cold, and hunger. Historians who have concentrated only on his need to win the war have criticized him as impractical, if not even indecisive, but Washington understood that the need of the hour was as much to win a whole people to the concept of revolution as it was to win the revolution itself. It was his breadth of vision, and his concern for human values, as well as his greatness as a man of honor, that made him one of the great generals of history.

If it is true even in the military that leadership means leading others, and involving them, not driving and coercing them, then how much more is it true in matters where total self-sacrifice is not the issue.

This book is written primarily for those who understand that more can be accomplished by working *with* people than *over* them.

Leadership is an art. Bad leadership is usually due more to clumsiness than to ill will. Leaving aside the natural bullies — most of whom, except in circumstances where bullying has been imposed as the norm, have neither the intelligence nor the perceptivity to earn positions of real authority — people who fail as leaders usually do so simply because they are ill at ease in positions of leadership. They are like the untrained singer who bellows loudly to conceal his inability to produce a pure tone; like the actor who bludgeons his audience with bombast because he hasn't learned how to win them with subtlety; and like the mechanic who, unable to find the malfunction in a motor, kicks it in the hope of starting something.

Any tailor knows you can't merely jam a thread through the eye of a needle. The strands must be brought carefully to a point, then inserted cautiously into the eye, allowing not a single one of them to escape.

The same is true of any art. One cannot bluster. One must attune himself sensitively to the requirements of the medium he is using. To paint fine lines, an artist must use a thin brush, not a thick one. To depict loneliness, a composer may well limit himself to a simple melodic line; certainly he won't use crashing chords.

Bluster, unfortunately, is the response of many people in positions of leadership to even sensitive issues, issues where finesse and patience are essential if the support of one's subordinates is to be won. At such times, especially, the temptation often arises to consider things more important than people. Often, indeed, in such situations, one hears the justification, "But it's a matter of principle!" Is it? Sometimes, perhaps. But even then, is not kindness also a principle?

My hope in this book is to help people in positions of leadership to see their roles, not as "big shots," but as artists whose medium is the dynamics of human cooperation.

Because the suggestions offered in these pages are people-oriented rather than job-oriented, they will prove helpful as well to anyone, whether in a position of leadership or not, whose lot it is to work with others: parents, for example, in raising their children; teachers interested in drawing the best out of their students; store salesmen seeking to interest their customers in the products they sell; or anyone wanting to win others to a point of view.

Even people who live and work alone may find suggestions in these pages for drawing the best out of themselves.

To recapitulate the rules given in this chapter:

1. Genuine leadership is supportive, not coercive.

2. The true leader tries to lead others, not to drive them.

3. Leadership means involving others.

4. Leadership means vision first and above everything; action, secondarily.

5. Leadership means understanding that people are more important than things.

6. Leadership is an art, to be learned and applied sensitively. It is not to be confused with mere position.

Chapter Two

Leadership Is Not an Ego Game

What does leadership mean to you?

Does it give you a thrill to think of others looking up to you, awaiting breathlessly your slightest, but ever-wise, decision; or leaping to carry out your least, but always-firm, command?

If so, you may have the necessary instincts to command a flock of sheep, or to hold determined sway over a band of cut-throats (each of whom will, of course, be merely biding his time until he can cut *your* throat and grab your position).

Yours will, however, be essentially a one-man operation. You will be able to accomplish little through others. Most of your time, probably, will be spent in grumbling over your subordinates' incompetence or stupidity, in arbitrating their petty squabbles, and in settling endless private grievances.

Your subordinates will be incompetent, no doubt. You will have discouraged competence in them as a threat to your own autonomy.

They will quite possibly be stupid as well. Who, blessed with any intelligence, would remain for more than a few weeks in the condition of mindless obedience that you impose on your subordinates?

Inevitably, too, they will squabble, for you will have reduced them to positions of insignificance not only in your eyes, but also in their own.

And they will brood endlessly on their petty grievances, whether real or imaginary, simply because you have never held before them any vision that might have lifted them out of themselves.

When people are not inspired to give of themselves, they revert naturally to thinking what they can get for themselves. For such is the state of the unregenerate ego: self-centeredness, and the unending query, "What's in it for me?"

Ego-centricity is invariably self-defeating. While it seeks only self-gratification, it closes off the very channels by which it might achieve true fulfillment: self-expansion, progress, and creativity.

If a leader glories in the importance of his position, he will infect his subordinates with the same attitude. Never will he be able to inspire in them the dedication which can bring a project to success. Everything he attempts to accomplish must eventually bog down in incompetence and — unless its sights are set almost at ground level — in failure.

For the tenor of every group endeavor is always a reflection of the spirit of its leadership.

I myself came to this understanding after trying for years to deny it. I had the job of organizing groups under the coordination of an international headquarters. My endeavor was to free those groups from uncertain dependency on any one leader. It was only gradually that I came to see that I had been working against a simple reality of human nature: Rules and procedures are no substitute for creative leadership. And it was then I realized that leadership means cultivating people, not abstractions.

For as the leader is, so will the group be. A good leader attracts good subordinates — or in some cases simply magnetizes them so that they become good. A bad leader, on the other hand, can dissipate the magnetism of even the best team. No one with spirit, moreover, would remain longer than absolutely necessary under the direction of anyone completely lacking in spirit.

Ego games are not so easy to dismiss as they are to ridicule. Arrogance, indeed, is the first temptation of leadership. Not to be so tempted, furthermore, is not even necessarily a good sign in a potential leader. For whereas arrogance may be—*must be,* in fact—tempered if leadership is to be effective, unwillingness to lead may simply be an inborn trait, and unalterable. One who cannot come to terms with the thought of being a leader is someone whose natural mode of self-expression can only lie in some other field of action.

Nor should it be supposed that a person's unwillingness to lead necessarily marks him as humble, or that another person's acceptance that it is his nature to lead marks him as egotistical. Admittedly, creative expression of all kinds requires at least some degree of ego-consciousness. It is by creativity, however, when rightly directed, that we can develop to our own highest potentials. It is in fact to our own greater self-consciousness that we owe our ability, as human beings, to raise ourselves, and to improve our material lot—a gift that is denied the lower animals. For only because of man's capacity to tell himself, "I want to improve my lot; I want to change myself," can he begin the long upward climb from the fogs of nescience to the crystal clarity of enlightenment.

What is important in every creative expression, including that of creative leadership, is not to allow one's creative flow to be blocked by the thought of "I." The ego itself must be used creatively. It is the very thought of "I" which first generates creativity: "A new product is needed by my company; let me try to invent one"; or, "I'd like to write a new song"; or, "I accept the responsibility for leading this army to victory."

The important distinction lies in the direction of one's flow of energy. If that flow is focused inward upon the ego, in the thought of one's own importance, it becomes contractive, and limiting. If on the other hand it is a radiation outward from one's self, it becomes expansive. The more powerful that outward flow, the more magnetic it will be — and, ultimately, the more self-transforming.

If one's concentration is on "I, the great inventor," or, "I, the great poet," or, "I, the great general," one's creativity will become blocked by the ego. But if, on the contrary, one's energy-flow is directed outward — toward the thing one wants to invent, or the song one hopes to write or the war one intends to win, one's creative energy becomes liberated, and the flow toward success is assured.

Leadership, then, must be focused on the job to be done. Your own role in the completion of a task should not be the focus of your attention, however vital that role may be to the task itself.

The greater one's mental emphasis on himself as the doer, the less he will be able to accomplish — whether as a leader or in any other capacity. The greater his mental emphasis, on the other hand, on the job to be done, the more likely he will be to succeed.

To recapitulate the rules given in this chapter:

1. Self-importance in a leader is self-defeating.

2. The spirit of a group reflects the spirit of its leadership.

3. The ego can be either a hindrance or an aid to creativity. It is an aid if its

energy-flow is toward the job to be done, rather than inward upon itself.

4. Remember, leadership is not an ego game!

Chapter Three

Leadership Means Responsibility

Genuine leadership demands a sense, not of glamour, but of responsibility. The true leader is concerned not so much with the opinions of others as with the truth, with getting a job done, with inspiring others to join him in working toward a worthy common goal.

This concern implies a willingness to assume the responsibility not merely for success, but also for failure; a willingness to take the risks himself, instead of waiting for others to take them (absolving him thereby of any blame!)

Most people are happy enough to take the credit for having been right, but few are willing to take the blame for having been wrong. The genuine leader is indifferent equally to praise and to blame.

There are times, indeed, when he knows that he must shoulder an undeserved blame — perhaps because others wouldn't be able to bear the weight of it; or perhaps simply to see an issue dropped as soon as possible, so that everyone can get on with the job.

One learns in the role of leadership that the only way to get a job done is to get people to stop *reacting*, as they tend especially to do when they are blamed, and to start *acting*.

In this sense, a leader must be like a good athlete. A skier, for example, hasn't time to think whether he *likes* a particular rough spot on the slope. His one thought is, "What shall I *do* about it?"

A captain on the battlefield can't afford to waste time thinking, "If only the enemy would stop shooting at us!" If they shoot, they shoot. He can't change that fact, so why lament it? His urgent need is to find ways for his men to avoid getting hit, while attacking with the greatest effectiveness.

A businessman trying to win a contract knows that it can be fatal to react too personally to his opponents. No one will be impressed with him, if he bases his bid, for example, on a show of resentment of the competition.

I remember receiving a letter one evening years ago that threatened disaster for a project I'd been working on for many years, one that was particularly important to me. Well-wishers, seeing the shock on my face, urged me consolingly,

"Come on out with us for a cup of tea. It will make you feel better."

"What do you mean?" I replied. "Who cares how I *feel* about this letter? All that matters is what to *do* about it!"

My hands were unsteady as I drove home that evening. The unsteadiness wasn't due to fear, however; I hadn't time for that. My concentration was wholly centered in the thought, "There *has* to be an answer: What is it?"

The crisis, as it happened, was overcome, though with only hours to spare. I doubt that it would have been met successfully, however, if even a small part of my energy during those weeks had been wasted on how I felt personally in the matter.

Leadership doesn't have to be unfeeling! The best leadership, indeed, is rooted in compassion, in kindness, in deep concern for the welfare of others. But to be most effective it must at the same time be liberated from personal likes and dislikes. One's feelings — and even more important, one's intuitions — will actually be the clearer and deeper for being impersonal.

Look to the longer rhythms. Don't let yourself be jostled by the importunities of the moment.

Equally important is it for a leader's actions to be self-generated, and not merely reflective of the actions of others. He cannot afford to be drawn into other people's definitions of the problems he confronts. In this sense, too, creative action is infinitely more important than blind reaction. It implies complete, *personal* acceptance of the responsibility for getting a job done.

For leadership includes finding creative solutions to problems, which means taking responsibility also for one's creativity.

The mediocre general may exclaim, "According to all the recognized treatises on warfare, our situation is hopeless. What choice have we but to surrender?"

But the great general will say, "The recognized treatises offer no hope. Let us therefore create new guidelines!"

Thus was the Battle of Waterloo won. Thus also, the Battle of Hastings. And thus, again, the American Revolution — which introduced unorthodox tactics borrowed from the American Indians.

Remember, then: Leadership doesn't mean glamour; it means responsibility. And responsibility means thinking in terms, not of credit or blame, nor of how one might *feel*, personally, in any given situation; it means focusing simply on getting the job done.

It means, finally, taking responsibility for finding creative answers, even when one has every excuse for finding none.

To recapitulate, then:

1. See leadership not in terms of glamour, but of responsibility.
2. Be not so much concerned with the opinions of others as with the truth.
3. Be concerned not with praise or blame, nor with your personal reactions, but with action, with getting the job done.
4. Concentrate on the longer rhythms in any project, not on temporary ups and downs.
5. Be as ready to accept responsibility for failure as for success.
6. Acceptance of responsibility means accepting the duty to find creative answers even when convention says there are none.

Chapter Four

Leadership Means Setting Aside Personal Desires

Have you ever imagined yourself as a person of limitless power — perhaps as the king or queen, or president, of a large country; or as the chairman of the board of some international corporation?

If so, how have you pictured yourself?

Have you seen yourself as someone finally in a position to get everything he ever wanted?

Such is the popular view of leadership. People look not so much to the responsibilities of leadership as to its privileges. Indeed, the pages of history are fairly littered with examples of people highly placed who took advantage of the trust that had been placed in them.

Think of the kings and queens who abused their power: of the tyrants like Nero and Caligula; of the unscrupulous schemers like King John of England; of the self-indulgent voluptuaries like the more notorious of the oriental potentates; of the weaklings like the last kings of France and of Russia. Such monarchs were never prone to give first, or indeed any, consideration to the public weal.

Nor are examples lacking in modern leadership: people who have taken advantage of their positions of high trust to gratify their own selfish desires. Leaving aside the numerous dictators and their quenchless demand for wealth, pleasure, and life-and-death power over others, there are countless other cases of people in more run-of-the-mill positions, such as in business or politics, who seem to have defined leadership purely in terms of self-gratification.

Nevertheless, our thesis is true, and those leaders who reject it are merely false leaders. Theirs is the pride that goes before a fall.

For the true leader is one who puts his personal wishes, not first, but last.

A famous example of such true leadership was Sir Philip Sidney, in sixteenth century England, who, though himself dying on the battlefield, and desperately thirsty from loss of blood, gave his water flask to a dying soldier with the words, "Thy necessity is yet greater than mine."

Subordinates will often quote their superior's directives in terms of his wishes. They will say, "Mr. Robinson *wants* us to do (so and so)." In fact, if Mr.

Robinson is at all worthy of his position, he will confine his wants, if any, to his private life. When on the job, he will think of it only in terms of what is needed to get the job done well.

As he expects his subordinates to be obedient to him, so he himself should try to be obedient to whatever the circumstances call for. Always he should ask himself, not, "What would I like?" but rather, "What do I feel is needed?" and, "What is right?" He might even phrase the question thus: "What is trying to happen here?"

On his ability to tune in *impersonally* to the flow of events depends in large part his skill in leadership.

For there is a tide in every activity that transcends human dreams and expectations. Great leaders recognize that they can only catch that tide at its height, and ride with it: They cannot create the tide. Leadership in this sense is somewhat like riding a surfboard — a sport which requires great skill and control, but always directed toward riding *with* the cresting waves, not independent of them, and never against them.

Desires, aversions, personal likes and dislikes — these are the static that interfere with a leader's clear receptivity to the intuitive guidance he is seeking.

While not allowing himself to be guided by his personal feelings, however, he must keep himself open at least to consider the feelings of others, especially those of his subordinates. This is, quite simply, the sacrifice of leadership. For the feelings of others must be recognized as a factor in the formula of "What is trying to happen here?" Unless he can win support for his ideas, the best project may amount to nothing, since there will be no one to give it sufficient energy for the project to succeed.

If he cannot win the support of his subordinates, especially, he may well have no alternative but to wait.

I knew someone who, over a period of years, created a series of charitable organizations. All of them were legal entities, complete with government-approved constitutions and by-laws. The only thing missing, and the reason he kept creating new institutions, was a working membership.

After years of presenting people with so many workable plans, he expressed his frustration to me one day.

"I've done all the groundwork for them," he complained. "Why don't they come forward and carry on the work?"

He failed to realize that not only are organizations made up of people, but that people are made up of feelings. Unless those feelings are enlisted, no organization can come into existence.

There is also another, and deeper, reason for keeping oneself open to the feelings of others. The leader who, in his determination to exclude his personal feelings from every reckoning, refuses to consider any feelings at all is likely himself to become a mere robot.

Leadership without feeling is in fact an ideal that we find held up to the modern public in countless novels and movies. It must, one supposes, be some people's ideal of leaderly perfection.

Think of all the steely-eyed sheriffs of Western romance; of the many square-jawed tycoons of industry; of the endless series of stern-visaged generals staring with pointed chins into the distance.

Think of the classic scene from what was probably every movie ever made during wartime in England: The officer sends a young soldier, deeply in love and eager to live his life fully, out on a virtually hopeless mission.

"That will be all, Jones," he says, dismissing him as he returns to his papers.

Jones turns stiffly and strides to the door. His hand pauses on the doorknob.

"Sir?"

"Yes, Jones?"

Another pause.

"Nothing ... Sir." Lifting his chin a little, Jones closes the door behind him.

Sir Philip Sydney didn't ignore his soldier's feelings when he gave him his water flask. The genuine leader is a person of genuine feeling. It is his compassionate concern for those under him, far more than any tactical brilliance he may show in the field, that wins him their support.

For his feelings are directed outwardly, in giving to others; and never inwardly, in taking for himself.

To recapitulate, then:

1. The true leader puts his personal wishes last, not first.
2. A leader should ask himself in every circumstance, not, "What would I like?" but rather, "What do I feel is needed?" and, "What is right?"
3. A good approach to every problem is to ask oneself, "What is trying to happen here?" One's skill as a leader is demonstrated by his ability to tune in impersonally to the flow of events.
4. Leadership requires openness to the feelings of others, and not insensitivity to them in the name of "getting on with the job." To a major extent, their welfare is the job.

Chapter Five

Leadership Means Service

Too much attention, generally, is given to the position, rather than to the function, of leadership. But once rank assumes importance for its own sake, creativity and meaningful progress grind to a halt.

Only a weak leader feels the need to wave his position before his subordinates. A strong leader, on the other hand, wins support for his position by using his authority to focus attention on the work to be done.

Because self-importance is the natural human inclination, a safe attitude for you, if you are a leader, will be to remind yourself constantly that the position of leader is not, in the deepest sense, any more important than that of the humblest follower. Both are simply contributing whatever skills they possess to the advancement of an undertaking.

Often, indeed, the subordinate, because of his freedom to specialize, is in a position to make a more visible contribution than the leader, whose job essentially is to work *through* others.

In leadership, a garland of humility is more to be prized than any crown.

Think of Mahatma Gandhi, who insisted on traveling in third class carriages on the train "because," as he explained to someone who asked him his reason for doing so, "there is no fourth class."

Of course, for a leader to be effective in his role he has little choice but to accept some, at least, of the outward symbols of authority. Otherwise he may lose some of the respect and cooperation that are due his position, and may even cease to be looked up to as the leader.

Part of the skill of leadership is knowing how many of the trappings of leadership one may safely ignore without risking the loss of one's followers' respect and cooperation. The stronger the leader, the fewer the symbols he will need. The weaker the leader, correspondingly, the more he will need. On the other hand, a relatively weak leader would be mistaken to rely too much on outward symbols, if only because their excessive number will only advertise the fact of his weakness.

Lord Nelson, of Trafalgar fame, used to refer to his captains as "a band of brothers." But it was because he commanded their complete respect that he could afford to be so inclusive.

By contrast, I knew a man who commanded no respect at all in his own home, but who tried ineffectually to assert his authority by shouting at every meal, "This home is my castle!"

Humility is a sign of strength, not of weakness. Humility is above all, and quite simply, truthfulness — self-honesty.

It is not the false modesty of one retreating shyly into the limelight. It isn't, in other words, the sort of "humility" that was expressed in the introduction written by a French archaeologist to a book by one of his colleagues. Praising the book, this scholar wrote, "The author's distinguished work was done at our direction, and under our constant supervision."

Humility means seeing everything quite simply as it is, with none of the emotional overtones of wishing that it be anything more. A job done is simply a job done. It is the egotist who looks around for applause.

Andrew Carnegie revealed this kind of humility as self-honesty when he attributed his great success in business to his ability to attract a good team of co-workers.

My father, Ray P. Walters, showed it too. Offered the Legion d'Honeur for his discovery of oil at Parentis, near Bordeaux, France, he replied completely sincerely, "It was teamwork that found it. The members of our team were all equally responsible."

Humility was a quality of Abraham Lincoln. Accused in court by his opposing attorney of being two-faced, he replied wryly, "I leave it to the honorable jury. If I had two faces, would I be wearing this one?"

Humility in leadership can be achieved also if one learns to view his role as a simple service to others. Indeed, this is the very essence of leadership: giving energy, not receiving it. And perhaps the surest way to ensure such an outward flow of energy is to think of oneself always as serving one's subordinates.

Finally, and (provided you have the faith) most helpful of all: See God as the doer. Give Him the credit for any good that you do. Offer your work as a service to Him.

To return to the subject of an earlier chapter, you will also find it easy, in this case, to give God the blame — not in a spirit of accusation, but in the thought that, if a project failed, maybe it did so for a good reason.

Indeed, those who look even-mindedly on both success and failure, and who give everything to God, generally find that all things, in some uncanny fashion, turn out for the best.

To sum up, then:

1. See leadership as only a job like any other.

2. Leadership means giving service, not receiving it.

3. Humility is more important in a leader than any medal for achievement.

4. Humility is self-honesty.

5. If you have religious faith, see God as the doer; view your work as a service to Him.

Chapter Six

Leadership Means Loyalty

We said earlier that it is easy to drive people, but difficult to lead them. No matter how good an idea, if the people you lead aren't ready for it they will obstruct your efforts to implement it, or else change it in some way to reflect what they *are* ready for.

Many an institution has died when some project, often quite worthwhile, was rammed down the throats of members who were unwilling, or unable, to swallow it. And many a leader has ridden to defeat under the standard of a beautiful theory which he preferred to reality.

People are more important than things. No matter how good an idea, if the people under you are not ready for it, respect their position. Work with them as they *are,* not as you would like them to be.

Be patient. Understand that it often takes time to bring people to new points of view. Reflect how long it probably took *you* to come to your new point of view, before you could present it to them.

To win loyalty from subordinates, first *be* loyal to them. Never demand loyalty of others. For true loyalty cannot be commandeered: It can only be won. Be concerned only, therefore, with being completely loyal yourself.

The same is true for love: Never demand love of others. Love them without worrying whether or not your love will be returned. One who gives love freely is, of all people, the most certain to receive it back — even a hundredfold.

In correcting someone, think not only of his *need* to hear what you have to say; think also of his *readiness* to hear it. Wait until the right time to speak, when what you have to tell him will do the most good. For if you speak at the wrong time, you may never get another chance: When next you raise the issue, he will be likely to remember only the inauspicious time when "You said that before."

Be loyal first of all to your own.

In a school where the students were invited to share in the administrative work, complaints (not necessarily justified) were made against one of the teachers. The headmaster, eager to win the students by showing his loyalty to them, immediately took strong action against the teacher.

Wouldn't the wise and more truly loyal thing to do have been first to inquire into the justice of the charges, and then, if possible, to work quietly with the teacher to correct her fault? By courting the students at the expense of his own staff member, the headmaster showed himself not actually worthy of anyone's loyalty.

Moreover, he demonstrated that he was an incompetent leader. For the teacher and her fellow staff members were, after all, members of his work force. They would, if he treated them right, remain with him long after that particular group of students had graduated. But without the continued support of his teachers, the school itself would cease to exist.

Yet how many bosses, the moment they feel a little displeased with something, take the brunt of their displeasure out on those who are least in a position to defend themselves: their subordinates!

Authority so exercised is disloyal, incompetent, and even cowardly.

To be given authority over others is to be placed in a position of trust. The wise leader will, if anything, bend over backwards to defend and support his own. For he knows that whatever good he may hope to accomplish for others depends first on the strength of his own team.

Remember, then, these rules on loyalty:

1. Work with people as they *are,* not as you would like them to be.

2. Work with things as they are, and not as you would like them to be.

3. Be patient. Understand that it takes time to bring people to new points of view.

4. To win loyalty, be loyal yourself first.

5. To win love, first give love, yourself.

6. In correcting someone, consider first his readiness to hear what you have to say.

7. Be loyal to your own, first.

Chapter Seven

Leadership Is Intuition Guided by Common Sense

The wise leader is more concerned with what *is* than with the way he would like things to be.

He is more concerned with what will work than with getting his mere opinions accepted.

And he is more concerned with truth than with merely being thought right.

He is not afraid of submitting his ideas to the test of reality.

It is a sign of weakness in a leader for him to pull rank, or to defend his ideas, under attack, with the argument, "I have more experience in these matters than you." True, there may be occasions when he has no other choice. It is best, however, that those occasions be rare.

For the wise man has no need to surround himself with an impenetrable mystique. And that, essentially, is what people are trying to create when they offer in their defense such "stone-walling" arguments as rank, or greater experience, or their age, or total endorsement from their superiors.

The endorsement of others, incidentally, whatever their rank, is one of the commonest, and generally also weakest, arguments one can offer in defense of a doubtful proposition. "Everyone says so"; or, "I've heard it from lots of people":

Such claims, when pinned down, seldom yield more than one supportive name; often, not even that.

A good proposal, rightly presented, will stand on its own feet. It is only weakened when the clinching argument is that it has been endorsed by others, especially if these supposed supporters are unnamed. And if others do in fact feel as it is claimed they feel, they deserve better representation than the mere statement that such is their opinion.

An appeal to popular vote is not, of course, the sort that leaders are likely to make. Those in authority are more likely, but just as unwisely, to lean on the approval of those with authority over them. In this case, it is those superiors whom they represent poorly.

A junior officer ought to have the conviction to win people by his own authority, which has been invested in him by his superiors. He ought not to lean weakly on the mere fact that they have given him his authority.

The claim to have the support of others — conveniently absent, and therefore unable to represent themselves — or the endorsement of one's boss — conveniently unavailable for comment — is nothing less than an attempt to close the door on any challenge to one's own authority.

A good leader knows that nothing can really be gained by squelching his subordinates. Even if, as is probable, he *has* had more experience, or *is* older, or *does* have the boss's support, he should demonstrate his right to his position of leadership either by appealing to sweet reason, or by the sheer magnetism of his own conviction.

Alternatively, should he fail to win people by these means, he might do well to search for a compromise, or to suggest some other solution that they will be able to understand and accept reasonably.

Discriminating supporters need to be cultivated. Their discrimination can be dulled if all they are ever asked to do is stand about, applauding your sterling abilities. A handful of such supporters are a thousand times more valuable to any worthwhile undertaking than a veritable horde of blind followers and "yes-men."

I have mentioned the tendency to surround oneself with an impenetrable mystique. There is another version of this tendency. It is the claim to some purely personal intuition. This is a claim by which people often seek to support views which they find themselves incapable of defending on rational grounds.

"I *feel* this to be true," is the usual expression, one that is met with universal exasperation; or, "I *feel* that you're all making a serious mistake."

Leaders are by no means the only ones guilty of this ploy. Browbeaten subordinates may resort to it also, seeing in it their only defense against a leader whose technique of leadership is to overwhelm his subordinates. In fact, however, any argument that paralyzes reasonable discussion is an invitation to disaster.

What is one to make of personal intuition? Certainly, it exists. Probably no major victory is ever achieved without it. There are people, moreover, who possess this faculty in greater measure than others. The best leaders almost always possess it in abundance, even when they exercise it unconsciously.

To demand agreement on the strength of your intuition alone, however, would be to bludgeon your subordinates into mindless obedience. You may be perfectly right in what you feel. They may know, too, from experience that you are probably right. Nevertheless, if you want to develop them into a team of discriminating and cooperative co-workers, you had better find some means of persuasion that they will be able to understand and relate to.

Even if you feel strongly impelled from within to a certain course of action, it is better to speak of this impulse to others only rarely. Instead, offer them sound reasons.

Or — perhaps better still — offer them a chance to respond from intuition themselves. State your case to them simply, without frills, and invite their response.

There is a certain power that accompanies truly intuitive feeling that often carries the day, even if one hasn't labeled the feeling "intuition." People will be the more inclined to accept what you say if you offer your ideas to them in such a way that they, too, can respond on this level. Thus, you will encourage them to develop their own intuitive powers.

For intuition *can* be developed —not by all, perhaps, but by many people — with practice. There is a certain feeling that comes when true intuition is at work, as opposed to the mere enthusiasms of imagination. Experience will enable one gradually to recognize the difference between intuition and imagination. Occasionally, on the strength of such experience, one will be able successfully to take even major risks. History is full of examples of leaders who did so, and won outstanding victories.

Again, if what one feels in a given situation is valid, others will be able to "tune in" to it and sense its validity, too. Intuition need not be a means of excluding others from one's thought processes. Moreover, it ought never to be used as such.

Certainly, however, the safest course generally would be to rely on common sense. For it is easy to err if one relies too heavily on intuition, and difficult to err if one checks every subjective feeling against objective realities.

What is common sense? Most people think of it as the voice of experience. Fools suffer, but do they learn from their suffering? A donkey repeats the same mistakes, no matter how many times his peasant beats him. For experience alone is no guarantee of wisdom. Often, indeed, people who claim to speak from experience are merely intoning a dirge for past failures.

The purpose of common sense is to test the claims of enthusiasm, but certainly not to squelch them. Common sense is too often mistaken for the voice of doom. Generally, however, people who claim to represent the voice of reason are merely saying, "We tried that, but it didn't work."

I have spent much time in Italy, where people have sought my counsel on diverse issues. How often their reply to a suggestion has been, *"Ma, e difficile!"* ("But, it's difficult!") It's that "but" that's the killer. One expects a challenge not to be easy. Experience alone, however, that isn't enlivened by creative imagination, too often inserts a "but" in the hope of killing all further discussion.

This is why common sense has been paired with intuition in this chapter. These two qualities must work together harmoniously. Alone, they endanger the success of any enterprise: common sense, because it can reduce all creative action to a state of rigor mortis; and intuition, because, if unchecked, it can lead to disaster.

Here, then, is a workable definition: *Common sense is the willingness to learn from experience.*

Why "willingness"? Why not "ability"? Because, the *ability* to learn from experience suggests more than common sense. Ability is an attribute of wisdom. But to have common sense means merely to be reasonable, and for a person to be reasonable it is quite enough, surely, that he be *willing* to learn from experience.

In willingness to learn, there is openness. Common sense, so exercised, doesn't close the door on opportunity. Nor does it insist that past experience close doors on whatever hasn't yet been tested. It searches the known for guideposts to the unknown. While exercising a necessary check on intuition, it also opens the doors to intuition.

Such willingness — the creative use of common sense — permits the gradual development of intuition, without allowing intuition to spread unchecked into flowery meadows of imagination.

The message of this chapter might be distilled into the following rules:

1. The wise leader is more concerned with what *is* than with what

ought to be.

2. He is more concerned with what will work than with mere opinions, even his own.

3. He is more concerned with truth than with being thought right.

4. A wise leader convinces by sound reason, or by the magnetism of his own conviction, but not by the mere outward authority of his position or past experience.

5. Discriminating supporters need to be cultivated, not merely impressed.

6. Be wary of supporting your proposals on intuitive grounds alone. Try to present your ideas in such a way as to invite intelligent response.

7. Always be guided by common sense.

8. *Common sense is the willingness to learn from experience.*

9. Common sense and intuition can be developed hand in hand, each offer-

ing its own type of clarity to the other. Common sense should check the suggestions of intuition. And intuition should inspire common sense always to look beyond the enclosure of the known to the open pasture of the unknown.

Chapter Eight

The Importance of Flexibility

It is not weakness in a leader to admit error. Nor is it weakness to agree to other ideas than his own. The wise man knows that the fear of being thought fallible is itself a proof of fallibility. Human nature, after all, *is* fallible.

But remember also: *Truth always wins out in the end.*

Perfection in human terms is not a thing. Nor is it a fixed condition. It is a *direction* — a direction from the less perfect forever toward that which is more perfect.

A good leader will avoid holding fixed ideas. He will realize that living situations, unlike buildings and bridges, are always fluid. Today's right direction may prove a wrong one tomorrow, perhaps once some present imbalance has been corrected.

Do not think merely whether a thing *ought to* be. Think whether, realistically, it *can* be. Adapt your actions to reality, not to theory alone, no matter how beautiful you may consider the theory.

Deal with every situation as a thing in itself. Try not to hold the consciousness of working under a cloud of precedents — except to the extent that precedents may vitalize the project you are working on with life-giving rain.

And try not to create too many rules. It has been wisely said that "Too many rules destroy the spirit."

Rules and precedents are, of course, much less trouble to work with than the daily flow of creative action. They kill the life, however, of any worthwhile venture.

It has been said that to be a good leader one must first of all be a good follower. Yet there are many good followers who will never make good leaders, if only because they haven't the courage to accept personal responsibility for a project's failure. It might be truer, then, to say that a good leader must first be a good *listener*. He must be motivated by what is *right*, and therefore willing to listen to, and—if fairly convinced—to adopt, other points of view, even if at first they seem in conflict with his own.

There is a simple key to learning flexibility: Learn to be centered in yourself. The skier whose movements proceed from his center is able to turn easily, whether left or right, at a moment's notice. It is the skier whose center is outside himself — one who has his energy preset to turn left, for example, when a moment later he finds he has to turn right — who is liable to fall and end up at the bottom of the slope with his clothes all covered with snow.

Strong leaders all have this ability in common. They are centered in themselves — not self-centered, in the sense of being selfish, but rather always at rest inwardly. This inward poise is one of the secrets of personal magnetism.

Weak leaders, by contrast, are always those whose commitment to specific lines of action renders them incapable of reacting creatively to new developments.

Flexibility means the ability to hear every knock of opportunity when it comes, and to answer it.

Try, then, to live by these principles:

1. Be willing to admit your mistakes. Remember, truth alone wins out in the end.
2. Keep your ideas of perfection fluid. Remember that perfection in human behavior is not a thing, but a direction.
3. Adapt your actions to reality.
4. Deal afresh with each situation as it arises. See it as a thing in itself.
5. Don't make too many rules, lest they destroy the spirit of your enterprise.
6. Be open to other points of view; they might prove better than your own.
7. Learn to be centered in your inner self, and at rest.

Chapter Nine

The Need for Action, Not Talk

The newly elected officials of a formerly corrupt city government were in a tizzy. It seemed to them as though all their constituents had conflicting theories as to how the city government should be reorganized, and each was shouting for the acceptance of his own theories.

"We can't possibly satisfy them all!" cried the councilors in exasperation.

"Never mind," said the new mayor, a man of experience. "All we need to do is give them a well-run government. If we do, their theories won't matter to them any more."

Such, in fact, proved to be the case. Once the citizens found the new tree of government bearing wholesome fruit, they no longer cared much how the tree was being watered.

How often one finds debate only confusing issues instead of clarifying them! At such times, almost any action is better than wasting further hours, weeks, or months arguing the best possible course of action.

Planning that facilitates action may indeed save weeks of work. But planning that shelves action indefinitely only discourages the flow of creative energy. Many a project has been started under such a burden of carefully detailed plans and weighty expectations that, like an overloaded plane, it never manages to get off the ground.

People who devote too much time to discussing what they intend to do almost never end up actually doing it!

In one case to which I was a witness, the planners were so eloquent about a project that many people became fired with their enthusiasm.

I was not among them, however. There had been too much talk, too many brochures, too many tours of the property for a project that didn't yet even exist.

As things turned out, the project failed. How could things have turned out otherwise? The reasons for its failure were simply these: too many beautiful dreams; and too little energy left over, after the dreaming, for constructive action.

The effective leader knows that an encyclopedia of good ideas is no substitute for even the least of those ideas put into actual practice. For, in the last analysis, the essence of leadership is *action* — not discussion, no matter how intelligent or convincing the talk.

In every deliberation there comes a point when the door to further discussion must be firmly closed, even if the subject has not been exhausted, even if it seems that the best possible solution has not yet been reached. This point is reached when discussion begins to block, rather than liberate, a group's creative flow. At this point almost *any* action, short of utter lunacy, will be better than no action at all.

Never allow a group's creativity to become stifled by an excess of words.

It may be argued that action, without careful deliberation, may prove not only hasty, but harmful. In fact, however, action itself often has a way of clarifying issues. Obviously, one shouldn't, figuratively, leap blindfolded off a precipice. But one should at least test the possible avenues of descent, instead of standing about, endlessly theorizing.

The most important thing in leadership is to keep the creative energy flowing. As long as it continues to do so, that flow will itself generate ideas. It will melt away obstacles, open up new possibilities, and create a host of undreamed-of opportunities.

Remember these rules, then:

1. Leadership means action, not merely good ideas for action.

2. Don't waste so much energy in planning that you have none left over for acting on your plans.

3. Action generates creativity.

4. Almost any action is preferable to prolonged inactivity, born of indecision.

Chapter Ten

Giving Support

The leader who fears strength in his subordinates is concerned merely with protecting his own position. Any work that he and they may be engaged in is certain to produce only negligible results. Indeed, it is likely that such a leader will find himself eventually alone, in full and unchallenged command of a sinking ship.

For leadership means strengthening the work of which one is the head, not weakening it. And this can only mean encouraging strength, not weakness, in one's subordinates. The wise leader knows that on the strength of his supporters depends the full effectiveness of almost everything he can hope to accomplish as a leader.

The weak leader, however, will think, "What if, once I strengthen them, my subordinates should cease to support me? What if, instead, they become my rivals?"

If one is a loyal leader, he will attract loyal supporters. Disloyal subordinates, moreover, finding no vacuum into which they can move, will soon leave.

A good leader, indeed, will not only develop strong supporters, but will encourage them to develop their own qualities of leadership. He will encourage them also to develop their creativity. For he will realize that, by delegating authority to others, he will only *increase* his own powers of accomplishment.

To win the support of others, one must first give *them* support.

I knew a man who had been newly placed in charge of a particular department in an organization. He came to his superior and asked him, "How do you see my responsibilities in this job?"

The superior, because he had faith in the man's abilities, replied, "I'd rather you defined your own responsibilities. Until you do so, you won't be able to develop full effectiveness in your job. Come back to me when you've thought them through. We'll both be in a position, then, to discuss the matter further."

That superior might not have given the same answer to other subordinates. Wherever possible, however, it is always helpful to encourage people to reach their own conclusions, even if not taking it so far as letting them define their own duties.

It is often wise, moreover, to encourage them to follow their own projects, as long as the broader aims of the institution are served, or at least are not injured.

Suppose, for example, you have an idea that you want carried out, but the person you have in mind for it has some other idea. Suppose, even, you don't consider his idea as good as your own. In fact, to put a cap on it, suppose you know his idea won't even work. If he is eager to try it, and if you think the broader work can handle what you see as a temporary detour, it may be a good idea to let him go ahead with his plans.

There is always the possibility, however unlikely it may at first appear, of his proving to have been right after all. But anyway, at least he'll have learned in the process.

Helping others to develop their own understanding is often more important than making a sale, or winning a contract, or scoring a victory.

Don't be afraid of allowing your subordinates to make mistakes. It is only by trial and error that certain lessons can ever be learned. One prominent industrialist attributed his own considerable success to a willingness to allow his subordinates to make their own mistakes, and to learn by them.

Don't ask too much of people. Isn't it foolish to expect perfection? Be willing to compromise. You will get the best out of those under you if you work with them as they *are*. Don't ask more of them than they are able to deliver. Alternatively, if you see a need to challenge them and make them grow, expand their horizons gradually. Don't force them to strip their mental gears.

The people in an organization should count more with you than the work they are doing. *"People are more important than things."* If you make your co-workers your priority, you will inspire them to do far better in their work.

Never domineer your subordinates. *Invite* their response. Suggest your ideas. Give them the freedom to accept or reject your proposals. If they are allowed to reach your conclusions at their own speed, they will be far more likely to get behind your ideas and implement them.

Try never to impose your authority. See if you can't win people to your way of thinking, instead.

A corollary rule, and one which I personally consider fundamental (although I doubt you'll find it in any other book on leadership), is this: Accept only as much authority as people are willing to *give you*. Even then, handle it sensitively, as a gift.

There was a system of government in ancient India that has never been tried in the West. They had monarchies, of course, not democracies. And kings were traditionally the sons of the rulers before them, as they were in the West. Kings ruled, however, by permission of their people. It was understood that if the people no longer wanted them, they no longer had the right to rule.

It seems to have been a good system, for it held ever before the king the truth that he was his people's servant, not their master by divine fiat, as Western kings claimed for themselves.

Something of that system might be incorporated effectively into every organization where leadership is required.

A good leader should also be willing to do the lowest and most difficult task. He should never assign jobs to others that he would not be willing to perform himself. Always, he should feel that it is his place to serve others.

Finally, he should always look ahead to the time when he will have to step aside and allow others to take charge. As all life is said to be a preparation for the "final examination" of death, so all leadership should be viewed as a preparation for that moment when one passes the reins to his successor.

On how well your organization functions *after* you leave it, quite as much as on how well it is functioning now, can your true skill as a leader be judged. It is a sad fact that organizations rarely continue to flourish after their founders' passing.

To reiterate, then:

1. Try always to strengthen your subordinates in their work, in their creativity, and in their qualities of leadership.

2. Encourage them in their projects.

3. Allow them to learn by their mistakes.

4. Be willing to compromise. Don't ask more of people than they are able to deliver; or, if you do so, stretch their

horizons gradually.

5. *Invite* their support; don't commandeer it.

6. Accept only as much authority as they are willing to *give* you.

7. Never assign any job that you wouldn't be willing to do yourself.

Chapter Eleven

Work With People's Strengths

As a leader, you will get the best results for the least amount of effort if you work with those who are in tune with your ideals. You would be wise not to give a disproportionate amount of energy to those who are not in tune. Creativity cannot thrive where too much effort is devoted to merely holding the line.

If you develop a nucleus of people who work well with you, and who work well together, others will be drawn in by the magnetism they generate. The stronger the vortex of positive energy, the greater the creative flow. This is the opposite teaching from the well-known saying, "A chain is only as strong as its weakest link." True, if you are working with a chain you'd better see that every link in it is strong. More often, however, you'll be working with vortices of energy. In this case, you'll only dilute their energy if you devote much time to negative vortices, which may seem more like black holes in outer space, drawing even the light rays inward to themselves, than like stars that emit light.

In working with individuals, too, concentrate on helping them to develop their natural strengths. Many think to help others by pointing out their weaknesses. Generally speaking, however, people improve more by magnetizing their virtues than by brooding on their shortcomings. In concentration on their faults they tend — again, like those black holes in space — to allow their energy to be absorbed by negative thoughts, such as discouragement and insecurity. Soon, there is no energy left for creative self-development.

Only in creative expansion of awareness is it possible to deal with inner weaknesses effectively. When a person is encouraged to concentrate on developing his strengths, they soon give him the positive magnetism he needs to give battle to his faults.

As a man of wisdom once said, "Don't try to banish the darkness by beating at it with a stick. Turn on the light, and the darkness will vanish as though it had never been."

Try also, as much as possible, to let a job grow out of the person himself — out of his nature and personality, out of his ability to handle the task, out of his special interest in it. Don't ever look upon him as a mere instrument for getting a job done.

In a large undertaking, it is impossible not to have to work more closely with some people than with others. Be impartial, however, in your respect and friendship for all.

Select those with whom you work closely for their qualities of selflessness, of putting the good of all ahead of their own personal interest. And then don't by-pass the lines of authority.

Don't worry too much about negative energy, if it arises — unless, indeed, you are conscious that a crisis is actually looming. For negativity, generally speaking, has little cohesive power compared to the magnetism that is generated by those who put out positive energy, and who set good examples.

If emotions become stirred up against you, the best course is not to counterattack. Reason, moreover, will not often work in your favor. For emotion, once aroused, abhors reason. Better wait, then, for emotions to cool — assuming that the issue can in fact be shelved for a time.

Meanwhile, go along with the feelings that have been aroused. Show people that you are listening to them, as indeed you should be.

A good technique, if you can manage it without sacrificing sincerity, is to tell them, "Maybe you are right." After all, to say so doesn't necessarily commit you.

If they want to confront you, take the initiative away from them if you can. They have no right to seize it from you. Call them in first. Say to them, "Maybe I've been wrong. Why don't we all see what we can do to improve matters?" In this way they, too, will have to accept the responsibility for improving matters.

But if it is clear that you are indeed in the wrong, take the blame onto your own shoulders before they have a chance to load you with it themselves. Again, however, try to enlist *their* energy in bringing about a correction. It may be possible thereby to help them to redirect their negative energy into more positive channels.

Exercise common sense in campaigning for what you believe in. Don't fight for a cause unless you stand a reasonable chance of winning. For even the pettiest defeat will be remembered by some people, and will weaken your authority with them on future issues.

If anyone has suggestions to make, try to get him to implement them himself. If he expresses criticism, ask him to propose solutions to the problems he sees. Then, if possible, assign him to carry out his proposed solutions.

It is easy to tell others how they ought to behave, or what they ought to do. But once the carping critic finds that by his complaints he is likely to draw more responsibility onto his own shoulders, he will be more likely to temper his criticisms with charity, and with practicality.

As for outright dissenters in your organization, give them, if possible, a chance to show themselves up — or, alternatively, to show themselves in the right, in which case everyone should be grateful for their suggestions. But if you don't give them this opportunity, they will continue to grumble, and their dissension to fester. For there will always be a few who will listen to them. No one will listen, however, once by their own actions they have proved themselves wrong.

At the same time, it helps to speak out against negative criticism in general. Urge people to mix with those in the organization who are interested in finding positive solutions, and to avoid those who would rather grumble than help.

Encourage the doers, not the talkers.

Where you see an opposite cause from your own winning, give in gracefully just as long as high principles are not at stake.

For to concede defeat gracefully is not really defeat at all, but a very special kind of victory — one for which people will honor you, and often far more so than for the times you were proved right.

Encourage those who are willing, rather than those who demonstrate unwillingness. For usually it is no specific request you make of people that renders them either willing or unwilling. It is some habit in them, a reactive mechanism they've developed for handling every challenge.

For yourself personally, fear praise more than criticism. For the snare into which too many leaders fall is not criticism, but flattery. Never court popularity. Be concerned rather with issues, with causes, with principles, than with popular acclaim.

In matters of leadership, never speak from your personal likes and dislikes, and especially not from a level of emotion. Speak from a sense of justice, of what is right and true. There is nothing so likely to win you disrespect from your subordinates as any uncontrolled display of emotion.

When dealing with individuals, put any prejudices you may have resolutely aside. Think of others with empathy, as their sincere friend — or as though you were perceiving them, not at, but *from* their own inner center. Try to reflect back to them that judgment, that advice, from their own higher self which they may be too confused to perceive themselves.

Remember, finally, that the best work is always done through inspiring people, never by driving them to work.

Remember these rules:

1. Work to strengthen a subordinate's best qualities, rather than harping on his worst. You will accomplish far more by encouraging others than by belittling them.

2. Work more with your organization's strengths than with its weaknesses. Channel more energy to those people in it who are in tune with what you are doing than to those whose tendency is to resist you.

3. Don't invest a disproportionate amount of energy in addressing negative situations. Strengthen the positive side, rather, and any negative vortices of energy that exist will tend either to be dissipated, or to remove themselves from the scene.

4. Don't allow subordinates to offer merely negative criticisms. Teach them that they must earn the right to speak by

offering solutions when they want to point out problems.

5. Encourage the doers under you, not the mere talkers.

6. Never court popularity for yourself. Be concerned with issues, with principles.

7. Never speak from your own emotions or private prejudices, but always from a sense of justice, fairness, and truth.

Chapter Twelve

What Is True Success?

A true leader is neither attached to success nor afraid of failure. He knows that success is not so much the completion of a specific project as the energy that goes into completing it. Projects can be destroyed, but never energy itself.

A good leader works as much as possible through others, not directly himself.

He is more concerned with winning the war, so to speak, than with winning battles. He is willing to compromise in little matters in order to win on the larger issues. He always keeps long, not short, rhythms in his labors toward success.

The definitions of success are legion, as are also the techniques for reaching it. The most important thing this book can add to those multifarious definitions and techniques is this simple rule: *The outcome of any project always reveals, however subtly, the kind of energy that went into its development.*

A work of art reveals not only the skill, but also the consciousness, the basic attitudes, the philosophy of life, of the artist.

A place of business reveals the general attitudes of its workers: their happiness or unhappiness, their confidence or frustration.

A leader who leads truly, and never drives others, will create in his subordinates the most constructive possible attitudes, and will ensure the best possible long-range results for his and their labors.

The true success of an undertaking depends more than anything else on the spirit of the people involved in it. And the spirit of those people is a reflection, always, of the spirit of its leader.

What is Crystal Clarity?

Crystal Clarity means to see oneself, and all things, as aspects of a greater reality; to seek to enter into conscious attunement with that reality; and to see all things as channels for the expression of that reality.

It means to see truth in simplicity; to seek always to be guided by the simple truth, not by opinions; and by what is, not by one's own desires or prejudices.

It means striving to see things in relation to their broadest potential.

In one's association with other people, it means seeking always to include their realities in one's own.